Judy Blume

The Library of Author Biographies™

JUDY BLUME

Cee Telford

rosen central™

The Rosen Publishing Group, Inc., New York

For Mouse the cat, who likes to sit on the keyboard
while I type

Published in 2004 by The Rosen Publishing Group, Inc.
29 East 21st Street, New York, NY 10010

First Edition

Library of Congress Cataloging-in-Publication Data

Telford, Cee.
Judy Blume / Cee Telford.— 1st ed.
    p. cm. — (The library of author biographies)
Summary: Discusses the life and work of this popular author, including her writing process and methods, inspirations, a critical discussion of her books, biographical timeline, and awards.
Includes bibliographical references and index.
ISBN 0-8239-4523-5 (library binding)
1. Blume, Judy—Juvenile literature. 2. Authors, American—20th century—Biography—Juvenile literature. 3. Children's stories—Authorship—Juvenile literature. [1. Blume, Judy. 2. Authors, American. 3. Women—Biography. 4. Authorship.] I. Title.
II. Series.
PS3552.L843Z9 2003
813'.54—dc21

                                                    2003009182

Manufactured in the United States of America

Excerpt from *Newsletter on Intellectual Freedom*, January 1983, p. 21, reprinted by permission of the American Library Association.

Text from *Principal*, "What Kids Want to Read," Volume 61, Number 3, January 1982, pp.6–7, reprinted with permission of the National Association of Elementary School Principals.

Table of Contents

Introduction: Judging Judy

It's hard to imagine the world without Judy Blume. Since 1969, when her first book was published, more than 75 million copies of her books have been sold worldwide. She is best known as the author of the hilarious "Fudge" books, which started with *Tales of a Fourth Grade Nothing* in 1972, and a number of more serious books for older readers, beginning with *Are You There God? It's Me, Margaret* in 1970 and *Then Again, Maybe I Won't* in 1971. She has now written more than twenty books and she shows no signs of stopping. Her most recent book, *Double Fudge*, was published in 2002.

In the majority of her books, the main characters are between ten and fourteen years old, and in fourth through eighth grades. To Blume, this transition between being a kid and being a teenager is one of the most interesting and difficult stages in life, and that's why she has continued to write about it throughout her career. Blume remembers this as a period of great emotional and physical change in her own life. Some of these changes confused and upset her, but she was too ashamed to talk to anyone about how she felt. She didn't want anyone to think she wasn't "normal." It made her feel very lonely. "You pretend like everybody else, I'm normal," she says, reflecting on her preteen years. "But inside you know you're not, [and] the harder you try to be. And you're afraid to be yourself because there is no yourself. You don't even know who yourself is."[1]

As a child, Blume looked to books for answers. She hoped that she would find her experiences and feelings reflected in stories she read, and that way, she would know she wasn't alone. But when Blume was growing up, all the stories for girls her age were mysteries or adventures or stories about horses. She enjoyed these books, but she felt something was missing. "Where were all the books about real kids with real feelings?"[2] she wondered. Blume never would have guessed that one day she would fill this vacuum—by writing realistic books about puberty and adolescence.

In the late 1960s, when Blume began writing, the world was ready for more realistic fiction for children. Attitudes were changing—people were talking more freely about sex, racism, and war than they had in the decades before—and children's literature was ready for a change that reflected that. Blume was there, ready to respond to the challenge.

After a modest reception of her first two books, Blume burst into the spotlight with the publication of *Are You There God? It's Me Margaret*. It was a book she'd been itching to write—the very book she wished she had been able to read as a twelve-year-old girl. With this book she established herself as one of the pioneers in a new era of children's literature—among the first to write "reality-based" fiction for young people.

For Judy Blume, writing realistic fiction requires being honest and telling it like it is, even when it's uncomfortable or awkward. She gets inside her characters' heads and lets us hear their thoughts, even when they are not saying these things out loud to other characters in the book. She shows how they experience the world rather than telling us. And she doesn't pass judgment or moralize by saying things are right or wrong. She leaves room for the gray areas and lets her characters make the decisions that are right for them as individuals by exploring their options.

She is not afraid to illustrate that growing up is difficult. Her characters struggle with the physical changes that come with puberty, peer pressure, feeling alone, sibling rivalry, the desire to be popular at school, crushes on the opposite sex, and first sexual experiences. She shows that kids are faced with tough physical and emotional changes, even under the best circumstances.

Being different in some way can exaggerate this even more, setting teenagers apart at a time when the peer pressure to conform is very intense. Judy Blume has tackled this head-on by looking at the experiences of kids dealing with being the new kid at school, being bullied, having a disability, or being of a different race from the kids around them. She also explores some of the changes that happen in life over which kids have no control. She looks at the powerlessness a young person feels when his or her parents decide to move or divorce or when a parent dies.

These are all tough issues—ones that Judy Blume doesn't tiptoe around. But while her commitment to honesty has made her one of the most popular writers for children, it has also gotten her into a lot of trouble. There are those who have tried to silence Judy Blume by banning her books from libraries and calling her work "garbage" and even "pornography." Banning books is a form of censorship—when people remove or suppress things they consider objectionable. By banning Judy Blume's books, certain adults are making decisions about what kids can and cannot read.

Blume's response to those who wish to remove her books has always been the same. She believes that young people should have the freedom to make their own choices and, furthermore, that "kids have a right to read about themselves," especially since "they've been denied that right for a long time."[3]

When Judy Blume first started publishing, there was a desperate need for books like hers. She became hugely popular because there was a real appetite for reality-based fiction. Her work was original and fed that appetite. Thirty years later, there are a lot more books out there for kids to read about other kids just like them, but Judy Blume remains hugely popular even though her books might seem less radical today. A generation has passed, and the children who were her first audience are now encouraging their own children to read her books. Blume's books touch on the essential and universal theme of the experience of growing up, which gives them staying power in the face of changes in language and technology.

1 Judy's World

Most of Blume's books are set in the place she knows best—suburban New Jersey, where she was born and mostly grew up. She was born Judy Sussman on February 12, 1938, in Elizabeth, New Jersey, the town where her parents also grew up. Her father, Rudolph, was a dentist, and her mother, Esther, like most women of her generation, was a stay-at-home mom. Judy has one brother, David, who is four years older than she.

Imagination

Judy was a sensitive child who felt things very deeply, particularly fear and confusion.

She describes herself as a small, skinny girl who, up until the fourth grade, was very shy and fearful. She was afraid of a lot of things, including the dark, dogs, and thunderstorms. She was also an imaginative child—often pretending she was a detective, a prizefighter, or a famous ballerina. Her biggest dream was to become a movie star, but the only person she shared this fantasy with was her father. Rudolph Sussman encouraged his daughter's big dreams and acted as both a friend and playmate to young Judy.

Her mother, Esther, was quieter and more serious than her father. Although she was emotionally quite distant, Esther encouraged other things in Judy, such as a love of reading. Esther herself was an avid reader. Their house was full of books, and Esther regularly took her daughter to the library. Judy was also encouraged to read by her favorite aunt, Aunt Francis, whom Judy called Fanta. Fanta was a school principal and read stories to Judy when she was little.

It wasn't hard to inspire Judy to read since she'd had a love of stories from very early on. She was always making up stories like the ones she heard on the radio—adventures, romances, and mysteries—and giving imaginary lives to her paper dolls. She became very attached to some of the characters in books. When she was young, Judy's favorite book was *Madeleine* (1939), Ludwig Bemelmans's famous story about a spunky little girl in Paris. She loved the book so much that she actually hid it in a kitchen drawer, pretending she didn't know where it was even though it was long overdue at the library.

Life Becomes More Uncertain

Aunt Francis, like most of Judy's other relatives, lived in Elizabeth and played an active role in her childhood. When she was ten, Judy's grandfather died, and this was followed not long after by the death of one of her aunts. Five years later, her grandmother died, and this hit her particularly hard. Learning about loss and grieving at such an early age led to Judy's profound fear that her own father would die. His two elder brothers had both died at the age of forty-two, and Judy was convinced that this would happen to her father when he reached that age.

Judy was afraid of death in general and wondered what it felt like to die. She began to think that the adult world must be full of other scary things, but she didn't know what these were and this made her anxious. She wondered what being grown up felt like. Rather than expressing these uncertainties by talking, she turned to books, trying to find answers within them.

Part of the reason she kept her feelings to herself was because Judy didn't want to upset her parents. Her brother had always been rebellious, constantly upsetting his parents with his behavior, and Judy wanted to be the perfect child—as unlike him as possible. Throughout elementary school, she was popular, did ballet, got As, and was never in trouble. She put so much pressure on herself to be perfect that, as she recalls, "I never felt that I could be sad or disappointed or even angry. I had to be Little Miss Sunshine all the time."[1]

She was sick a lot of the time—with stomach-aches, mostly—and this seems to be related to the fact that while she had shared her earlier fears with her parents, by the time she was ten, she was keeping a lot of things to herself. She must have feared that displaying anything that might have looked negative would cause her parents to withdraw their love. She lived in fear that her father would die after all; perhaps the fear of being abandoned by her parents in any way was just as strong.

She certainly felt very scared when she was faced with separation from her father. This happened when she was ten. Her parents decided to rent an apartment in Miami Beach because her brother was sick with a kidney infection and they felt the Florida climate would be better for his recovery. Her father had to stay behind in New Jersey to operate his dental practice, but they would be together again on holidays.

At first, she hated Miami Beach and resented having to be there. Being the new kid at school, she was initially shy, but she gradually made friends both at school and in the neighborhood and became more outgoing. She even brought together some friends from her ballet class to put on a performance for the people in her apartment building. She organized the whole show—from choreographing the dances to making the programs.

Judy came to love all sorts of things about Miami Beach—being able to play outdoors all the time, going to movies with her mother, ice-cream sundaes, and the beach. She even taught herself how to swim, overcoming something she had been afraid of up until then. Overall, she became more adventurous during that time in

Miami Beach. Perhaps that's why as an adult, she speaks of those two years as being the most memorable years of her childhood. And as they were heading back to New Jersey, Judy realized with huge relief that her father was now forty-three. Her worst fear had not come true. Her father was alive and well, and now they would all be together again.

On the Verge of Adolescence

By the time Judy returned to school in New Jersey, she wasn't a little kid anymore. She was twelve, and she and her friends were developing new interests—like boys. While they were in Miami Beach, Judy's dad had built her and her brother a rec room in the basement of their house in New Jersey, and once they were back, her parents agreed that Judy could have a party and invite both girls and boys. This was the first of many parties that would be held in the Sussman rec room over the years. In grade six, it was mostly talking, eating, games, and goofing around. Later, the rec room was the setting for many first kisses.

Judy and her girlfriends spent a lot of time talking about boys. She and her best friends,

Rozzy, Ronne, Nancy, and Anne, formed a secret club in sixth grade called the Pre-Teen Kittens—devoted to discussions about the boys they liked. They were also preoccupied with how their bodies were developing, comparing notes on underarm odor and body hair. They had a lot of questions, especially about menstruation. When Judy tried to find answers in books, she found some technical information, but her biggest questions were ones about how having your period feels. Could everyone tell when you had your period? Did you feel more grown up having it? She didn't find answers to these questions in the books she was reading.

Comparing herself to her friends, she thought she was a late developer. She was humiliated by the fact that she was more flat-chested than they were and wasn't wearing a bra yet. Whether she needed it or not, she bought a bra, but then she had to stuff it with cotton balls to make it look like there was something there. She was the last among her friends to get her period, too. At one point, so eager to start, she pricked her finger with blood and smeared it on a pad that she then wore just so she'd know what it felt like when the time came.

When Life Becomes Art

Judy Blume didn't know then that these incidents in her own life—even the smallest details—would later show up in her books. She didn't yet know she was going to be a writer. She certainly loved to make up stories in her head, but it's a big leap from there to becoming a writer. It's hard to imagine a career as a possibility when you have no role model or real, live example.

Later, when Judy did become a writer, she had access to a wealth of material straight from her own life. In *Starring Sally J. Freedman as Herself* (1977), for example, ten-year-old Sally has just moved to Miami Beach with her mother, grandmother, and brother, leaving her father behind because of his job. Sally spends a great deal of time worrying that her father will die. But Sally finds friendship and happiness in Miami Beach. She becomes more outgoing and even organizes her friends to do a public dance performance.

In *Are You There God? It's Me, Margaret*, Margaret Simon forms a clique called the PTSs, or Pre-Teen Sensations, with three other girls. Humiliated by being such a late developer,

Margaret stuffs her double-A padded bra with cotton balls and prays to God to hurry up and bring her her period.

While these two books are clearly Judy Blume's most autobiographical, bits and pieces of her life and the places she has lived are scattered throughout all her books. This is due in large part to her incredible memory. Even as an adult, she claims to remember pretty much everything from the third grade on—exactly what she was thinking and feeling. With this kind of access to the past, it's no wonder Judy Blume has the ability to render details so accurately that her books seem real.

2 Becoming a Writer

Judy was, in many respects, a typical teenager. She was even a lucky teenager, because her parents were pretty easygoing and many of the best parties were held at their house. The early games in the rec room had become more serious by the time Judy was in junior high. There were lots of kissing games going on in the basement, and there was plenty of opportunity for flirting and fooling around with boys. Her parents gave Judy and her friends plenty of privacy, and by the time she was fourteen, her brother was out of the way, too, having gone off to college.

With its jukebox and grand piano, Judy's house was a popular place for hanging out.

Judy loved music. In high school, she sang in the choir and took modern dance. She also worked on the newspaper. Like the rest of her school activities, she excelled at journalism, and after two years as a reporter for the school newspaper, she became the editor, a job she shared with her best friend, Mary.

When she was fifteen, she met an older boy—a sophomore in college—named Bernie. They dated on and off for six years, although it was all pretty innocent. Her parents let her date: she was allowed to stay up as late as she wanted provided she came up to their bedroom and let them know when she was home and that she didn't "park" with boys. "Parking," a term that was used in the 1950s, meant driving to some secluded place and pulling off the road with the intention of fooling around.

Judy dated a number of different boys and went steady, but she never felt pressured by Bernie or anyone else to do anything she wasn't ready to do. The one time she and a date pulled off the road into a wooded reservation to "park," a policeman pulled up beside their car and asked Judy how old she was. That certainly killed the passion—she never tried parking again.

"I was usually in love,"[1] recalls Judy, but like her girlfriends, she kept quiet about her sexual experiences. Because "nice girls didn't" in the 1950s, there was a lot of shame about sex even though it was probably on everybody's mind.

Judy graduated from high school with high honors. She could have gone to any college she wanted, but in the end, she chose Boston University for the simple reason that she had heard that the university was full of boys.

University

For middle-class white women of the 1950s, going to university was usually a way to find a husband. Judy Blume had always been a good girl, doing what her parents expected of her, so despite the wilder dreams she had had when she was younger, she set about doing what she believed she was supposed to do—go to college, get married, and have children. In that order. As she recalls:

> I went to college to be a teacher because I was influenced by my mother's practical wishes for me. I knew my goal in college was to meet a man and get married. My mother said to get a degree in education in case I ever had to work, but I wasn't really thinking. I

was very busy wanting to get married and have babies and play grown-up.[2]

Teaching was seen as a suitable profession for young women of the time, but if women worked, it was expected that they would give up their jobs upon marrying. Marrying was the real job, after all—marrying and having babies.

While Judy set out to study education at Boston University, her career there didn't last long. In the first semester, she came down with mono (mononucleosis, known as the "kissing disease") and had to be sent home on a stretcher to recover. She was sick for months and decided to go to school somewhere closer to home.

When she reflects upon it now, Blume wonders if she wasn't a bit of a hypochondriac—someone who suffers from imaginary illnesses—when she was younger. A person's imagination can actually be so powerful that he or she can become physically ill, but being a hypochondriac is usually a sign that something else is wrong. She'd had repeated mysterious stomachaches when she was a child, but the source of this discomfort was probably not physical. As the "good daughter," getting sick was perhaps the only way she could get the attention she needed. Interestingly, after her first book was published, more than ten years later, Blume never again suffered from any serious illness.

After recovering from mono, Judy started classes at New York University. It was 1957, and it was an exciting time: the students were very bohemian and wore long hair and beads and talked about poetry and politics and art. Although she enjoyed participating and dressed to fit in by wearing black turtlenecks and corduroys, at heart, Judy was probably more conservative than the independent and carefree students she encountered in New York. When she went home for the holidays, she dressed the part of the good girl again, changing back into sensible sweater sets in pastel colors.

Marriage and Motherhood

Back home, at a party one Christmas, she met a young man named John Blume who had just graduated from law school. Before long, she started having happily-ever-after dreams at the thought of him. In December 1958, after a year of dating, Judy and John were engaged. The marriage was to take place the following August. Judy's brother, who was stationed in Libya with the U.S. Air Force, flew home that summer for the wedding. It seemed like such a happy time for the family, but Judy's worst nightmare was about to come true. Suddenly, her father died of a heart attack—the very same night his son arrived home. He was only fifty-four years old.

Twenty-one-year-old Judy and twenty-seven-year-old John had a quiet wedding in the shadow of her father's death. It was very difficult for her. Judy missed her father terribly, and she felt guilty for spending more time with her new husband than her grieving mother. But then again, her mother wouldn't talk about her father's death. It was a time of silence and internalizing feelings. John, too, Judy recalls, wasn't much of a communicator.

They settled into married life after about a year. John was working at his father's law firm in Newark, New Jersey, and Judy was still working on her degree at NYU. When she graduated with her teaching degree in 1960, Judy was pregnant with their first child, a daughter named Randy who was born the following February. Before she got pregnant, she'd been planning on teaching second grade, but now she had to put her teaching career on hold. Two years later, in 1963, their son, Larry, was born.

Beyond Marriage and Motherhood

The Blumes moved to a bigger place just before Larry was born—a suburban ranch-style house in Scotch Plains, where the kids could each have their own bedroom. Blume remembers being happy at the time. Here she was, a wife and mother with a house in the suburbs. She was living the American dream. But a few years into this comfortable existence, she began to feel that something was missing in her life—she needed an outlet for the creativity she had put into music, dance, and journalism in high school. She missed the exchange of ideas and the exposure to art and politics she'd had at NYU.

There was little to inspire her in suburban New Jersey. She was bored, and she was often sick. It was the 1960s, and great changes were happening in the world, but there she was, living in what she remembers as "the most deadly, apathetic [emotionless], uninvolved place on earth."[3] In suburban New Jersey, people weren't engaged in the big debates that were happening in the United States—the fights against racial discrimination, the protests against war—and

27

they weren't using poetry, art, and music as ways of expressing themselves.

Blume was desperate to be involved, but when she looked around her, she saw no other women working outside the home. All of the women she knew were homemakers. Blume didn't have big political ambitions, but she did want to do something creative. There was a lot of talk about empowerment in the 1960s—particularly for women—and she wanted to do something that wasn't about pleasing other people. She felt she'd spent her whole life trying to please others—first her mother, then her husband and kids.

Because her kids were still young, she came up with ideas that she could do at home. The first was to try her hand at songwriting, though she gave this up when she realized she couldn't come up with anything original. Then she started making felt banners to decorate children's rooms, and while she had some success with this, it was painstaking work and she became allergic to the glue she was using.

Next, she turned to making picture books. Her kids were five and three, and she'd been reading them lots of books and making up other stories for them while she washed the dinner dishes. She started to write the stories down and accompany them with her own illustrations. She sent these out to publishers and received rejection letter after rejection letter. Despite the fact that this upset her, she kept trying. "Please let me be published," she would go to bed praying. "I don't even care if they pay me. Just let me be published."[4]

Then she saw an ad for a writing class, and this really sparked her interest. She enrolled in the class called Writing for Children and Teenagers, taught by the famous children's writer Lee Wyndham (author of *Candy Stripers* [1958] and *Beth Hilton: Model* [1961], among other books) at NYU. Traveling to New York for an evening class once a week and learning about writing and publishing totally excited Blume. She worked hard and began to have some success with the publication of a few of the short stories she'd written for class. Then came a real triumph—she got a call from someone at the publisher Reilly and Lee saying the company was interested in publishing her first book—*The One in the Middle Is the Green Kangaroo*. It was a picture book about a boy named Freddy Dissel, who feels he's ignored because he is the middle kid in the family.

Blume recalls being "overjoyed, hysterical, unbelieving"[5] upon hearing this news. Unfortunately, her husband, John, didn't share her enthusiasm. He thought jobs were only about money. She was paid $350 for that first book, and he thought that was way too little money for so much work. But for Blume, it wasn't about the money, and this was something he couldn't understand. Ironically, just as Judy Blume was discovering her voice, her marriage was beginning to deteriorate.

Neither she nor John could have realized it at the time, but Judy Blume was about to be catapulted into the spotlight; she was on her way to a hugely successful career. As she would later recall: "That was the beginning of what's been a long and exciting adventure. Writing changed my life forever. It may have even saved it."[6]

3 Growing Up with Judy Blume

After Reilly and Lee published her picture book, *The One in the Middle Is the Green Kangaroo*, in 1969, Blume sent a manuscript called *Iggie's House* to Bradbury Press. She'd read that they were looking for realistic fiction for young people, and *Iggie's House*, which she'd written chapter by chapter in her writing class, seemed to fit the description.

Iggie's House

Iggie's House is about the arrival of a black family, the Garbers, in an otherwise white suburban New Jersey neighborhood. Winnie, a white girl in grade five, goes out of her way to try and befriend the three Garber kids. Other people in the neighborhood are less welcoming— one woman actually circulates a petition asking people to agree with the "suggestion" that the Garbers might be happier moving somewhere else. Winnie is very naive, thinking that she can simply counter the racist attitudes of the other people in the neighborhood through friendship.

She tries to show the new kids that she is aware of racial issues by asking if their father took part in the race riots that happened in Detroit the year before. The kids are offended and remain justifiably suspicious of her. Does she think all black people participate in riots? And is she only interested in being friends with them because they are black?

The Detroit riots were a real event. So was the assassination of Dr. Martin Luther King Jr. in 1968. Racial tensions were running high in the late 1960s when Blume wrote *Iggie's House*. She wanted to explore the ideas of racism and racial equality. Although Blume's intentions were good, *Iggie's House* was panned by the critics. They found it simplistic, lacking a sophisticated or in-depth understanding of the complexities of racism.

Finding Her Voice in Margaret

Funnily enough, before the critics had their say, Blume already knew that *Iggie's House* wasn't a great book. The criticism certainly hurt, but she didn't think the book reflected what she was capable of doing as a writer. When she had first met editor Dick Jackson at Bradbury, he hadn't accepted the manuscript right away. He discussed it with her, asked her a lot of questions, and sent her away to revise it without offering a contract to publish it. When he received the revised manuscript, Jackson was impressed enough with it that he was then willing to offer her a contract.

Blume was, of course, very happy that *Iggie's House* would be published, but she was even more keen for Bradbury to have a look at a new novel she was working on. She'd already formed a good working relationship with Dick Jackson, and he and his partner, Bob Verrone, were very taken with her description of the new book, which was about a twelve-year-old girl growing up with questions about religion, sex, friendship, and puberty. Her publishers knew it was a risk—no one had ever written a book like this for kids—but it was an exciting risk, and one they were willing to take.

Blume knew that kids talked about these things with each other, so why not see them written down? *Are You There God? It's Me, Margaret* was an easy book for her to write. As she recalls, "I just let go and wrote what I wanted to write and told the truth about what I felt."[1] Blume had no trouble remembering what it felt like being twelve, and she drew a lot from her own experience.

The story begins just as Margaret, the main character, has moved from the city to the suburbs. It's still the summer holidays, and she's anxious about starting sixth grade at a new school. Luckily, she makes friends that summer, which helps ease the transition. Her new friends even include her in the formation of a secret club at the start of the school year. Margaret keeps asking God to speed up her development so she can be just like her new friends. The funny thing is, Margaret doesn't know who God is. One of her parents is Jewish but the other isn't, and they leave it up to her to choose a religion. As much as she prays to God to bring her her period, she prays that God will also bring her a religion.

Although Blume was pleased with the book—she felt it was written from her heart—she braced herself for bad reviews from the critics because of her experience with *Iggie's House*. She needn't have worried, though. The *New York Times* loved it and later named it one of the best books of the year for children.

But despite all the positive praise from the critics and from kids who read the book, Blume angered a lot of adults. First, there were those who didn't like the fact that Margaret's talks with God are funny. Because religion is usually treated as such serious and somber business, they thought Margaret's talks were disrespectful. But underlying the humor, Blume is exploring serious issues, like the fact that Margaret's family is divided by religious difference. Her mother's parents never accepted their daughter's marriage to a Jew, and as a consequence, the extended family is divided.

This was mild criticism, though, in comparison to the reaction there was to Blume writing about menstruation. There were plenty of people who felt that it was a little too honest to be talking about a topic like this, and they demanded that the book be taken out of school libraries.

Then Again, Maybe I Won't

With the success of *Are You There God? It's Me, Margaret,* Blume knew there was a need to keep on telling stories in which the simple truths of the lives of teens and preteens were laid bare on the page. Dick Jackson at Bradbury encouraged and supported Judy Blume's work, even if and when it made some adults angry.

Her next book, *Then Again, Maybe I Won't,* was published the following year—1971. This time, Blume was interested in exploring the issue of puberty from a boy's perspective. This book also begins with a move—Tony Miglione's family moves from a working-class Jersey City neighborhood to a wealthy Long Island neighborhood after his father gets rich from patenting an invention. Tony isn't entirely comfortable with the changes that happen in his family now that they suddenly have money to spend. His parents seem ashamed of things that seemed normal before— like the fact that his father drove an old truck with his name printed on the side and that Tony's grandmother lived with them and did all the cooking. He has to find a way of fitting in to his new environment while not "selling out," like the rest of the members of his family.

Meanwhile, he has got puberty to deal with—he's feeling a lot of guilt and shame about his sexual feelings. First of all, he has started having wet dreams; second of all, he gets the occasional erection at school. Third, he has been spying on his sixteen-year-old neighbor, Laura, watching her undress through a pair of binoculars. There's no one he can talk with about any of this. Certainly not his father, who tries to bring up the subject of sex with him.

"You see Tony . . . there are things you should know about girls and babies and about . . . look Tony, do you know anything? . . . Tony . . . I asked you, do you know anything?"

"Sure Pop," I said.

"You do? You know about babies . . . how they're made?"

"Sure Pop. Since third grade."

My father looked like he couldn't believe it. "Since third grade?"

"Sure Pop. Big Joe told me all about it."

"You're positive you have the right information?"

"Sure Pop."

"Do you know other things too, Tony?"

"Sure Pop. A lot."

My father looked relieved.[2]

Deenie

In many ways, what Blume was doing in the 1970s was breaking the taboos against talking to kids about sex. She continued to do so with the publication of *Deenie* in 1973.

Deenie is the story of a fourteen-year-old girl who develops scoliosis, a curvature of the spine, and has to wear a back brace. Blume's idea for the book began when she met a woman at a party who was distraught because her daughter had just been diagnosed with scoliosis. Blume was later surprised to discover that the woman's daughter actually had a very positive attitude and was able to speak frankly about her feelings. This inspired Blume to do some research on the subject.

In the book, Deenie is under a lot of pressure to be beautiful. Her mother wants her to be a model, but with the diagnosis of scoliosis, her mother's dreams are shattered. This doesn't make it any easier for Deenie to accept the fact that she's going to have to wear a brace that extends from her neck to her hips. Neither does the fact that her mother continues to deny that anything is wrong with her daughter, saying things like, "No one in my family has ever had anything like this."[3]

Some mothers of readers have been angry about the portrayal of Deenie's mother. She comes across as extremely selfish. But her selfishness is an important part of the story. This isn't a book about scoliosis but, as Blume has always insisted, one about a girl dealing with the pressure of her mother's expectations.

Blume has admitted that the fathers in her books are probably more sympathetic characters than the mothers because she was closer to her father than her mother. In most of her books, the fathers are loving characters, but they are often rather ineffectual or even bullied by their wives. As Deenie's sister, Helen, says: "Ma really burns me up sometimes . . . I wish Daddy would tell her off just once!"[4]

Deenie's story is inspiring in large part because Deenie rises above her mother's expectations. By educating herself and her friends about scoliosis, Deenie finds a way to accept her fate, while her mother continues to deny it. Despite her condition, she is accepted by her peers because she accepts herself and has a positive attitude.

Deenie is a normal teenager who is dealt a bad blow. She is otherwise popular, pretty, and interested in boys, and occasionally she masturbates. This last fact had some critics praising Judy Blume for her courage and others calling for the book to be banned. Blume wanted to include masturbation in the book because, as she says, "If I could have read *Deenie* at 12, I could have known that other kids masturbate and God I would have been relieved."[5]

There have always been myths that masturbating can result in disaster. Deenie hears some of these myths at school—"that boys who touch themselves too much can go blind or get very bad pimples or their bodies can even grow deformed."[6] She begins to wonder whether touching herself has anything to do with her scoliosis. The gym teacher sets Deenie and her classmates straight with a frank talk. As Mrs. Rappoport says: "It's normal and harmless to masturbate . . . Nobody ever went crazy from masturbating but a lot of young people make themselves sick from worrying about it."[7]

"Private Books"

Are You There God? It's Me, Margaret, Then Again, and *Deenie* are among Blume's most popular books. Kids have sought them out because they speak about things that a lot of adults don't seem comfortable talking about—including parents and teachers. As Mark Oppenheimer wrote in the *New York Times*: "It's quite easy to understand why teachers don't assign Blume to schoolchildren. What teacher wants to risk being the first adult to discuss masturbation with a room of 11-year-olds?"[8]

Blume has never wanted her books to be referred to as "the one about menstruation," "the one about wet dreams," "the one about masturbation," and so on. She thinks of the books as being more complex and dealing with a number of different issues, including the recurring themes of moving, making new friends, and feeling isolated and confused. In *Deenie*, for example, she says she didn't set out to write a book about masturbation. It was just something that emerged as she developed the character, and it's certainly not the main theme of the book. But the fact is, many kids, many parents, and many adults who read the book when they were younger remember the books in this way.

Blume doesn't mind that her books are not usually assigned classroom reading. She thinks of the act of reading one of her books as an intimate exchange between herself and her readers. She says: "I feel very strongly that some of my books are private books . . . books that I see as a little visit between me and the child reader . . . I don't think kids should be made to talk about every book they read. There should be books kids don't have to answer questions about."[9]

4 Relationships

As Blume published more and more books, an increasing criticism of her work by teachers and critics was that she always set the stories in comfortable middle-class suburban environments. After all, not all kids have such privileged backgrounds. She has defended this by saying that she writes about the world she grew up in, the world she knows best. It is because this environment is so real to her that she can portray it so effectively to her readers.

Many of her books illustrate that young people living in middle-class suburban neighborhoods still have to deal with the same issues of being uncomfortable and embarrassed at puberty. And, furthermore, in places like the privileged New Jersey suburb where Blume lived with her husband and children, things weren't always as perfect as they looked from the outside. Divorce was becoming more common. Blume could see how worried her children were when couples in the neighborhood split up.

When Larry and Randy asked their mother whether this would happen to their family, too, Blume tried to reassure them, but as she later admitted in *Letters to Judy* (1986), she wasn't really sure. On one level she knew that her own marriage was in trouble, but on another level she was choosing to deny it.

Writing About Divorce

In order to answer some of her own and her children's questions, she wrote *It's Not the End of the World* (1972). The main protagonist, Karen Newman, is in sixth grade and her parents are splitting up. She and her siblings have different responses to this: Karen tries to bring her parents back together, her older brother acts out his anger, and her younger sister has anxiety dreams. Karen keeps hoping for a miracle, but she has to accept the fact that there is nothing she can do: her parents won't be getting back together.

Blume wrote about divorce again fifteen years later. She wanted to show that divorce is always painful, even if it is more accepted and common today than it was in the early 1970s. In *Just as Long as We're Together* (1987), the main character, twelve-year-old Stephanie, is faced with the harsh reality that her parents are splitting up. She doesn't share this news with her best friends, Alison and Rachel, because she is in denial about it to a large extent, as if not speaking about it will make it go away. It almost costs Stephanie her friendship with Rachel: Rachel has a suspicion that Stephanie's parents are splitting up and feels very hurt that Stephanie won't share this with her. After all, they're supposed to be best friends.

It costs Stephanie in other ways as well. She is angry and confused, and instead of talking about her feelings, she overeats as a way of comforting herself. This is a common theme in Blume's books—if you suppress your emotions, they are bound to come out in other ways. This message is perhaps made clearest in *Then Again, Maybe I Won't*. Tony Miglione suffers mysterious stomach cramps. He gets them after his new friend Joey shoplifts things; he gets them when he sees the changes that wealth brings in his parents' lives. Eventually, a psychiatrist helps Tony get better, simply by allowing him to talk about how he feels.

Changes in Blume's Life

Blume claims she was still in denial when she dedicated *It's Not the End of the World* to her husband, John. Just a few years later, they were divorced, too. This was a very hard time for everyone in the family, but they made it through and went on with life.

In 1975, she and the kids moved to Princeton, New Jersey. Randy and Larry couldn't understand why their parents had to live apart, and while Blume knew it would be the best thing in the long run, she was afraid of facing the world as an unmarried woman. Being married had been central to her identity. It wasn't a bad marriage, but in the last few years she had felt like she was dying inside. She was no longer the girl John had married. Her writing career had allowed her to grow, and she was seeking more growth—changes that marriage to John just wouldn't accommodate. In some senses, she says that leaving the marriage was a form of rebellion against the role she felt other people expected her to play.

As rebellious as she might have been, though, Judy was lonely without John. She was also a terrible romantic. It didn't take long before she met someone else and fell in love. Tom Kitchens was a physicist, and he was also divorced. A few months after they met, he moved to London, England, to work temporarily. Judy and the children followed. They moved back to the United States later that year, and Judy and Tom got married. She and the children moved to Los Alamos, New Mexico, moving again to the place where Tom had a job.

For Blume and her children, it was a painful time—she was unhappy with the marriage, and all of them were unhappy in Los Alamos. The whole relationship had happened very fast. Judy and Tom had both been lonely and eager to love again, and in retrospect, Blume felt it probably should have been a brief relationship rather than a marriage. In 1979, after three years of marriage, they were divorced. Blume and her two children remained in New Mexico, moving to Santa Fe, while Blume also kept an apartment in New York.

All of this moving and the change of partners was especially hard on the kids. Larry was sixteen and Randy was eighteen by the time Judy and Tom divorced. When she looks back on it now, Blume laments: "We've gotten through it somehow, but it certainly wasn't easy for them. I look at my kids and I think how I've disrupted their lives so many times!"[1]

Living with Teenagers

Blume admits she made mistakes with her kids, like everybody does. One thing she *was* able to do for them was offer them stories. When Randy became a teenager, she read a lot of romances for teens, but she was disturbed by the fact that they always turned out badly. She asked her mother to write a realistic novel, not one full of heavy moral judgment.

In response to her daughter's request, Blume wrote *Forever*, a love story about two responsible teenagers. It was published in 1975, when Randy was fourteen. In the novel, the main character, Katherine, is lucky enough to have parents who understand that teenagers fall in love and experiment with sex, and they give her the freedom to make her own choices.

Katherine and Michael are both high school seniors when they meet and fall in love. After months of heavy petting, they discuss whether to have sex. On the subject of sex, Katherine's mother says:

"It's up to you to decide what's right and wrong
. . . I'm not going to tell you to go ahead but I'm
not going to forbid it either. It's too late for any
of that. I expect you to handle it with a sense of
responsibility though . . . either way."[2]

Michael and Katherine promise to be
together forever and do eventually decide to
have sex. Katherine even goes on the pill. Sex
becomes a part of their relationship, and they
learn a great deal about trust and responsibility
because of it, and, as a result, they both mature.
Although the relationship comes to an inevitable
end, the experience has left them much better
prepared as adults to deal with relationships
seriously and responsibly.

The *New York Times* called *Forever* "a
convincing account of first love."[3] Many adults
today fondly remember *Forever* as the first book
they ever read about teenagers having sex.
When the book was published, though, there
weren't separate young adult sections in
libraries and bookstores, so it was shelved with
the adult books because of its sexual content. In
some ways, the categorization of the book is
arbitrary: Blume feels that anyone who is ready
to read it will read it—whether they are ready at
twelve or twenty.

Tiger Eyes

Blume wrote one other book for young adults—
Tiger Eyes, published in 1981. Like *Forever*, it
deals with love and sex between teenagers, but
this time in the context of a more complicated
story. The book begins with the funeral of
fourteen-year-old Davey's father. His death was
violent—he was murdered by a man who held up
the 7-Eleven store where Davey's father worked.
Davey, her mother, and her brother are living in
terror that the man will come back for them.
They need a break, so they go to Los Alamos, New
Mexico, to stay with Aunt Bitsy and Uncle Walter.

Davey feels utterly alone and is having
trouble coming to terms with her father's death.
Through new relationships, particularly one with
a mysterious young man named Wolf, she begins
to find a way to overcome her fears and discover
joy in life again.

Blume didn't really write about her feelings
about her father's death until this book. Although
Davey's father dies in very different circumstances,
both fathers die suddenly, and Blume modeled
Davey's reactions upon her own experience. In
Davey's relationship with Wolf, Blume is writing
about the healing power of love.

Judy Blume's "Forever"

Fortunately for Blume, the next chapter in her personal life was "forever." She met someone she felt she wanted to spend the rest of her life with. In 1987, she married George Cooper, who is also a writer. She became a stepmother to George's grown daughter, Amanda. During their first few years together, Judy and George lived in New York in an apartment overlooking the Hudson River. Now they divide their time between New York; Key West, Florida; and Martha's Vineyard. Blume is philosophical about her first two marriages, and she's very close to her children. Larry (now forty) is a filmmaker in New York, and Randy (now forty-two) is a pilot for a major airline. Judy and George are also the proud grandparents of Elliot, Amanda's son.

5 Censorship

Some of Blume's books have earned her bad reviews or negative reactions. While that can be difficult for a writer to deal with, censorship is another matter altogether. Censorship occurs at a number of different levels. A parent ripping pages out of a child's book; a school librarian, teacher, or principal deciding certain books aren't suitable and removing them from the shelves; religious leaders lobbying to have certain titles removed from schools; or a school board deciding that certain books won't be available in any of the schools in a certain town or state—these are all examples of censorship. Ultimately, censorship involves certain people making decisions on behalf of others. In the case of a writer for children like Judy Blume, censorship means adults making decisions about what children can and cannot read.

Blume heard stories about individual reactions to her books in the 1970s, like the one about a mother who was so offended by the passage on wet dreams in *Then Again, Maybe I Won't* that she cut the two relevant pages out of her twelve-year-old son's copy. Blume's books were even banned at her own children's school. She gave the school three copies of *Are You There God? It's Me, Margaret* when it was published. They never put the books on the library shelves because the principal decided that menstruation was an inappropriate topic.

But while isolated cases like these happened in the 1970s, this was a much more liberal decade than the 1980s. As Blume recalls:

> [A]lmost overnight, following the presidential election of 1980, the censors crawled out of the woodwork, organized and determined. Not only would they decide what their children could read but what all children could read. It was the beginning of the decade that wouldn't go away, that still won't go away

almost twenty years later. Suddenly books were seen as dangerous to young minds. Thinking was seen as dangerous, unless those thoughts were approved by groups like the Moral Majority, who believed with certainty they knew what was best for everyone.[1]

Since 1980, Blume has been one of the most frequently censored novelists in the United States. The books that seem to cause the most amount of commotion are *Deenie, Forever, Blubber,* and *Then Again, Maybe I Won't,* though it seems almost every one of her books has been labeled offensive by someone at some point or another.

In one case, after a school board in California removed *Deenie* from the shelves in 1982, it decided to put a general ban on all Blume books until the board could review each one. One board member went as far as to say, "Some of these books are pornography . . . We might as well put *Playgirl* and *Playboy* magazines in the library."[2]

Blume never set out to provoke people. She simply wanted to write honest books. And this principle of writing honestly is one she has stuck to. She was not about to let the censors stop her.

What things are the people who wish to ban her books reacting to? As Blume says in the introduction to her edited collection about censorship, *Places I Never Meant to Be* (1999), it's primarily three things: "lack of moral tone," strong language, and sex and sexuality.

"Lack of Moral Tone"

Blubber (1974), a book about bullying, is constantly being removed from the shelves because certain adults don't like the cruelty it describes. Worse than that is the charge that the book doesn't take a moral stand against this cruelty. The victim of the bullying is eleven-year-old Linda Fischer, an overweight girl in fifth grade. Wendy, a girl in Linda's class, is a born leader; she's clever but also cruel and manipulative. She picks an easy target in Linda because Linda never sticks up for herself. Wendy leads the class in bullying Linda, whom they nickname Blubber, after she gives her fifth-grade report on whales.

Jill, like the other kids in the class, goes along with the bullying because it's better to be on Wendy's good side, and as she says, "There are some people who just make you want to see how far you can go."[3] Even the singing teacher seems to feel this way—at one point she pulls some of

Linda's hair out, even though Linda doesn't appear to have done anything wrong.

The harassment Linda endures includes constant teasing and humiliating incidents like being made to strip down to her underwear in the girls' bathroom. When Jill challenges Wendy during a mock trial in the classroom, Wendy turns on her. Jill becomes Wendy's next victim, but Jill has the guts to fight back in a way that Linda never does. It's a painful and realistic portrait of the cruelties kids can inflict on each other and how the chosen victim can change in a second.

There are plenty of parents and teachers who didn't like *Blubber* when it first came out and plenty who don't like *Blubber* today. They don't like seeing children portrayed as capable of such cruelty; they don't like the explicit language the kids use; they don't like the fact that the book doesn't moralize and say "cruelty is wrong"; they don't like the fact that the teachers don't intervene and stop the bullying; and they don't like the suggestion that it's not just the fact that Linda is overweight that makes her a victim but that she somehow invites the bullying by not standing up for herself.

Blume actually feels *Blubber* is mild in comparison to real life. She saw plenty of cruel behavior among kids in the school yard when her own kids were young, and she also witnessed how disturbed her daughter, Randy, was by the bullying of a girl in her class when she was in fifth grade. Randy wasn't directly involved, but bullying creates a climate of fear—after all, anyone could be the next victim.

Mild or not, many school administrators called the book dangerous. They wanted a clear moral stand, one that offered a definite sense of right and punished whoever did wrong. But there are two problems with calling for a moral stand: Everybody's moral stand, or definition of right and wrong, comes from a particular perspective. But there are many different perspectives, resulting in many different moral stands. Second, sometimes things are more complicated than simply right or wrong.

People who demand that Blume take a moral stand in her books believe that children need to be directed toward the right answers and that, without guidance, they will be led astray. But Blume leaves room for children to make their own moral judgments. She obviously believes that young people are quite capable of determining right from wrong without any adult telling them. This is echoed in letters she receives from children.

In fact, one eleven-year-old girl wrote to Blume saying that kids *do* know the difference between right and wrong. She went on to say that she had never done something she hadn't set out to do because of a book.

Strong Language

Swear words will always get a reaction from certain adults, even though all kids know the words and most kids use them. *It's Not the End of the World* has been banned repeatedly because in one of the fights between the mother and father, the mother calls the father a "bastard." This entire book is therefore not available in some places because of one single word. But the word is spoken in the context of a fight between two people who are divorcing. Blume obviously felt it was a realistic word for the situation.

Blubber contains three mentions of the word "damn" and plenty of name-calling. This, combined with the perceived lack of moral tone, has made *Blubber* one of the most banned books of the last twenty years. The same is true of *Forever*. While the book is for young adult readers, some people still feel the language is too offensive. It contains many four-letter words, but probably none that would come as much of a surprise to a teenager. Blume defends the book by saying that the language is realistic; kids hear it and use it all the time.

Sex and Sexuality

The greatest anger toward Blume's books, though, has arisen in response to her frank discussions about puberty and sex. Some people seem to fear that reading about sex and sexuality will give kids ideas. It's emotional territory. Some people think sex education is a parent's job, while others think it is the school's job, and still others think it is the job of the church. Whoever's job it is, many, many people are uncomfortable talking about these issues, and everybody seems to have a different opinion on how much information is too much.

Apart from *Blubber*, the Blume books that are most often banned are the ones dealing with sex and sexuality. These are very obvious targets. There's the menstruation in *Are You There God? It's Me, Margaret*, the masturbation in *Deenie*, Tony's wet dreams in *Then Again, Maybe I Won't*, and Katherine and Michael's premarital sex in *Forever*.

These are all books about maturing, and they deal with sensitive topics, issues often surrounded by embarrassment and shame. Children have a lot of questions and concerns about these issues, and when censors ban books that deal with them, it's as if they are trying to erase reality. As Blume says, with censorship beginning in the 1980s, "Puberty became a dirty word, as if children who didn't read about it wouldn't know about it, and if they didn't know about it, it would never happen."[4]

Margaret, in *Are You There God? It's Me, Margaret*, is in sixth grade. There are plenty of fifth- and sixth-grade girls who have their periods, yet there are people who ban girls of this age from reading the book by keeping it out of schools and libraries.

Masturbation is an even more controversial subject, especially where it concerns girls. Blume recounts a story about one principal who asked the librarian at his school to keep *Deenie* off the shelf because Deenie masturbates. "It would be different if it were about a boy," he told her. "That would be normal."[5]

Tony Miglione, in *Then Again, Maybe I Won't*, luckily knows about wet dreams because he has heard some of his friends talk about them. When he has his first one, he knows what it is, although this doesn't make him feel any less ashamed. For some young male readers, *Then Again, Maybe I Won't* might be the first time they discover a name for what they are experiencing. For young females reading the book, it might offer them some insight into the issues boys their age are dealing with. But plenty of parents and school administrators have decided that it would be better if the book wasn't on the shelf.

Forever has been consistently banned from both junior and senior high schools because it involves teenagers having sex. Everyone has an opinion on when people are old enough to have sex, but Blume has argued that children actually start thinking about sex much earlier than adults like to admit. And in many cases, kids know a lot more than adults give them credit for. Remember Tony's father's surprise when he tells him he has known how babies are made since third grade?

Some people want the book banned for religious reasons. Some religions don't sanction sex before marriage. Added to this, there is probably also a reaction to the fact that Katherine goes on the birth control pill and, at one point in the book, says she would have an abortion if she got pregnant. Both of these are controversial issues from a religious perspective.

Blume's Response to Censorship

Blume has always received letters from her young readers, and she still gets hundreds a week. In many of them, kids ask her if they are normal and if she can explain the things their parents can't or won't. It's clear that kids are looking for information. As one twelve-year-old boy wrote to Blume: "How can they expect us to learn anything if they don't let us read stories that tell about life the way it really is."[6]

Blume feels that it is important to allow children to make their own choices about what they read. She believes children are smart enough to know both whether a book is right for them and when it is right for them. If the issues in a book seem too "adult" to a child, either they are not interested because they don't relate to it or they feel they are not ready to read it yet.

At the root of the desire to prevent children from reading certain books is fear. Parents who want to see these books banned are either afraid to talk to their kids about what they are experiencing or worried that reading them will plant ideas in kids' minds. This suggests that parents and children are having difficulty communicating. That's precisely why Blume established the KIDS Fund in 1981. The KIDS Fund gives support to organizations that work to encourage communication between parents and children.

Blume accepts that some people might not tolerate her books, but she says, "You can tell your own children what they're not allowed to read, and maybe that will work, and maybe it won't. But you can't tell everybody else's children what books will be available. It doesn't work that way." She points out that "if every individual with an agenda had his/her way, the shelves in the school library would be close to empty."[7]

To prevent this from happening, Blume has become an advocate against censorship and has spoken widely about the issue. One of her contributions to this effort is the book *Places I Never Meant to Be*, which she edited. She invited prominent authors whose work has been censored or challenged, including David Klass, Norma Klein, Julius Lester, Chris Lynch, Harry Mazer, Norma Fox Mazer, Walter Dean Myers, Katherine Paterson, Susan Beth Pfeffer, Rachel Vail, Jacqueline Woodson, and Paul Zindel, to contribute an original story. The book was published in 1999, with all proceeds going to the National Coalition Against Censorship, which has been and continues to be very supportive of Blume.

6 Thirty Years of Blume

Most of Judy Blume's groundbreaking books were published during the 1970s. A 1982 poll showed that Judy Blume was the most popular children's writer ever. The *American Library Association Magazine* asked thousands of readers across the United States to choose the fifty most popular children's books of all time. The results were astonishing.

1. *Superfudge*
2. *Tales of a Fourth Grade Nothing*
3. *Are You There God? It's Me, Margaret*
4. *Charlotte's Web*
5. *Blubber*[1]

With the exception of *Charlotte's Web*, the E. B. White classic about a pig and a spider, four of the five books were by Blume. This is something of a mixed blessing. There are people who question the quality of something if it is too popular. Although Blume has won more than ninety awards for her books, she has been passed over for many of the more literary awards because her work is seen as "too popular." Many of the awards she has won, though, are ones where young readers choose their favorite books. To Blume, those are the awards that matter most.

Writing for Different Reasons

Not all of Blume's books have been big hits. *Tiger Eyes*, for example, was something of a sleeper, and *Starring Sally J. Freedman as Herself* is a novel that kids either relate to or don't. *Sally* is set in Miami, in the late 1940s, just after World War II. It is the only one of her books that is set back in time, and it refers to a particular war that some readers have trouble relating to.

Judy Blume was born during that war, and even though she was only seven when the war ended, she remembers the feelings it aroused in her. In World War II, Jews were victims of

Nazism, and Blume was Jewish. How could she be sure as a child that a war like this wouldn't happen again? For Blume, writing *Sally* was obviously important, as it addressed certain issues that had preoccupied her for years.

She speaks of *Sally* as her most autobiographical book, and perhaps the need to tell her own story is why she wrote the book. It is the book closest to her heart, even though it is the one that is the least popular. Like many writers, Judy Blume writes different books for different reasons.

The Fudge Series

Some of Blume's books are written purely to entertain. Where almost every one of her books for middle-grade and young adult readers have provoked some controversy, the Fudge books seem to get universal praise from critics, kids, and their parents. The books are hilarious—full of slapstick humor and memorable silly incidents, although serious issues like moving and sibling rivalry underlie them.

Collectively, the Fudge books form a series starring ten-year-old Peter Hatcher, his troublesome little brother (a toddler called Fudge), and his archenemy Sheila Tubman. The Fudge series is largely modeled on Blume's son, Larry, as a toddler. In the first book, *Tales of a Fourth-Grade Nothing* (1972), poor Peter has to deal with the fact that he has a bratty little brother who's driving him crazy. Fudge throws temper tantrums, smears food on walls, scribbles on Peter's homework, and gets away with it all. Everyone thinks Fudge is simply harmless and cute, but Peter knows the truth. Later, in *Superfudge* (1980), Peter, then twelve, learns that his mother is having another baby! He can just imagine it—Fudge times two.

There's a girl at Peter's school named Sheila Tubman who also drives him crazy. Sheila follows Peter around and seems to have a lot of confidence. While she's a minor character in *Tales*, she's the star of the next book in the Fudge series, *Otherwise Known as Sheila the Great* (1972). Underneath that obnoxious exterior, Sheila is actually a very fearful little girl. In *Fudge-a-Mania* (1990), Peter's stuck spending the summer with the person he likes least in the world when the Hatcher family shares the rental of a summer house with the Tubmans.

Judy Blume's Writing Process

Blume has recently added a fifth book to the Fudge series, *Double Fudge*, published in 2002, which instantly made it onto the *New York Times* Bestseller List. But why another Fudge book after so much time? Blume never expected to write another Fudge book, but she has a ten-year-old grandson, Elliot, who has been asking for more adventures of Fudge for years.

Two generations have now inspired the Fudge books. It has been a long time between each book because these are not books Blume plans. That's because humor is one of the hardest things to write. It has to come naturally; it can't be forced. Blume usually finds that it grows out of a funny situation.

The Fudge books are different from her other novels, which she says require writing and revising many drafts over a period as long as three years. The books begin, in some way, long before she begins typing. She keeps a notebook and begins to sketch characters for months before she begins a book. She writes down anything that might fit in the story, like snippets of dialogue or descriptions.

When she sits down to begin a book, she has certain bits and pieces. She likens writing the first draft to laying out the pieces of a puzzle. By the third draft, she has put the pieces together to form a picture. With certain drafts, she needs to put the pages away and revisit them after a break. With fresh eyes, she can see new things. She also finds new insights and ideas when she reads her drafts aloud.

Remaining Relevant

Over thirty years, Judy Blume has developed certain patterns in her writing process. There are patterns in her books, too—a consistent style and recurring themes. The world has changed a lot since Blume's books were first published, but she has managed to remain both relevant and popular. Dr. Donald Gallo, a past president of the Assembly on Literature for Adolescents, once said that her popularity stems from the fact that "what she writes about and how she writes it make her characters and their actions more real than anything anyone else writes—or perhaps has ever written for preteenagers and younger adolescents."[2]

Blume believes that while some things change over time, like technology and the way kids use language, there are other fundamental things—primarily feelings—that are universal. In 1986, Blume published a collection of letters she had received over the course of twenty-six years, called *Letters to Judy: What Your Kids Wish They Could Tell You*. The collection shows that regardless of when they were born or where they live, kids are concerned with the same things and have very similar feelings. In exploring the feelings of kids and teens, Blume's books, even the ones written thirty years ago, remain very much alive.

Interview with Judy Blume

The following is an excerpt of an August 2002 interview of Judy Blume by Cynthia Leitich Smith. The interview is posted on Smith's Web site, http://www.cynthialeitichsmith.com.

CYNTHIA LEITICH SMITH: Judy Blume is the author of numerous books for readers of all ages, from picture books to middle grade and teen novels, to fiction for adults. Her titles include: *Are You There God? It's Me, Margaret*, *Blubber*, the Fudge series, *Forever*, and *Summer Sisters*.

On your Web site—judyblume.com—you mention that your ten-year-old grandson, Elliot, was the inspiration for your new title.

Does being a grandma give you a different perspective on childhood or children's literature? If so, how?

JUDY BLUME: Being a grandparent is wonderful! I love it. But I don't think it gives me a different perspective on childhood or children's literature. It does help keep me in close touch with today's children. But I think most of us who write for children find ways of keeping in touch with the current generation. We're all observers. We all listen carefully. We're genuinely interested in kids. Otherwise we wouldn't write for and about them.

CYNTHIA LEITICH SMITH: I often interview my characters, ask them to write letters to one another, do background reading, and read through my entire manuscript again after I write each scene. I'm increasingly looking for ways to trick myself into letting a story cool off between drafts. What is your writing process like?

JUDY BLUME: I keep a notebook for months before I actually sit down to begin a new book. Before I start the notebook I have a vague idea of the characters and their story, usually something that's been brewing inside my head, sometimes for months, sometimes for years. I jot down anything that comes to mind during this period—details about characters, bits of dialogue, chapter ideas, descriptions—sometimes even scenes. This way, when I actually begin, I have my "security blanket."

I find that when I'm doing a first draft it's important for me to keep going. Otherwise I get into revising each scene a million times and never move ahead. What works best for me is to get a first draft down as spontaneously as possible. It's very rough and I always think, if I die now this will never be published. No one will have a clue what it's about. I don't need to cool off between first and second drafts. A first draft for me is getting the pieces to the puzzle, the second draft is trying to make sense of the pieces, the third draft is painting a picture using the pieces, and all drafts after that are improving the picture.

I like a cooling off period between the second and third drafts and again, before I send it to my editor. It's amazing how much you see when you've put the manuscript away for a couple of weeks, even a month. Then—and this is so important—I'll read the manuscript out loud. I guarantee, by reading and listening, you'll want to make so many changes. A young novelist (two books published) was telling me recently that next time, he wants to record his book before it's copy edited. Me, too!

CYNTHIA LEITICH SMITH: Many writers describe themselves as "character" or "plot" writers. Which are you? What do you find to be the hardest part of writing?

JUDY BLUME: I'm a character writer but there wouldn't be a book if that character didn't have a story to tell. I tend to get ideas about a character in a situation. I don't like to think about "plot." I don't know everything that's going to happen when I begin. I know where I'm starting and where I'm hoping to wind up (though that sometimes changes along the way). The hardest part of writing for me is getting that first draft. I find it pure torture.

CYNTHIA LEITICH SMITH: In a recent interview on my Web site, An Na (who won this year's Printz award for *A Step from Heaven*) wrote, "Thank God for Judy Blume or else I would have no clue about sex or my body. None of that got discussed at home, which I think is the case for so many other teenagers." Adults lie to children or omit information all the time, yet you are forthright and honest through fiction. At first, was that a scary thing to do? Did you close your eyes and worry about irate grown-ups?

JUDY BLUME: I didn't worry at all. I didn't even think about it. I was young and naive and nobody told me what I could or couldn't write. I was writing about what I knew to be true because I remembered it so clearly.

CYNTHIA LEITICH SMITH: Did your editor ever question your content? This may seem like a strange question, but with so many grown-up gatekeepers, how did you manage to put young readers first?

JUDY BLUME: When I started writing in the late sixties (*Margaret* was published in [1970]) the gatekeepers were in their dormant period. I've often said the seventies were a very good time for children's books and those of us who wrote them. So many of us started out at the same time—Richard Peck, Rosemary Wells, Norma Klein, Harry and Norma Fox Mazer, E. L. Konigsberg, Robert Cormier (and those are just a few of us).

It's not that you put young readers first when you're writing—not consciously, anyway. You get into that place where you're writing from deep inside. You just want to tell the best stories you can. With me, I wanted to be honest—maybe because I felt grown-ups hadn't been honest with me when I was a kid.

My editor questioned content only once, during the height of the '80s book banning craze. It involved a line or two in *Tiger Eyes* in which Davey, the protagonist, allows herself to feel again, after her father's death. I've written about this incident in the intro to *Places I Never Meant to Be*.

CYNTHIA LEITICH SMITH: A lot of writers— at various career points—struggle with rejection, unsupportive friends or family members, mixed reviews, and their own insecurities. Our first instinct may be to think that writers like you are strangers to these sorts of feelings.

JUDY BLUME: Ha! I've never met a writer at any stage of his/her career who doesn't deal with insecurities. Just before *Summer Sisters* was published I begged my husband to help me buy it back from the publisher. I convinced myself it was going to be a disaster, the end of a wonderful career, and I didn't want to go out that way. He suggested I leave the country instead. I didn't. But I did keep an "anxiety diary" during my promotional tour. You can find it online at my Web site under "Summer Sisters." I reread it from time to time to remind me—not that I need reminding. The happy ending to that story was that *Summer Sisters* became my most successful book. So, you see—I'm no stranger to such feelings. I'm a stranger to feeling secure.

As for reviews, what can I say? Negative ones hurt. But you get over them. I have one "friend" who always calls after a negative review is printed in the *New York Times* or some other publication she finds at the doctor's office or the hair salon and says, in a funereal tone, "I saw your review." Maybe she thinks this helps me feel better. It doesn't. Good reviews, on the other hand . . .

CYNTHIA LEITICH SMITH: What would you like to say to writers who are reading this interview and wondering if they can keep creating, if they are good enough, if their voices and visions matter enough to share?

JUDY BLUME: Stop thinking about it. Your job is to focus on the book you're writing. You have to chase those demons away or you'll never do it. Not that I don't go through it myself these days. But when I began I didn't know enough to scare myself. So I wrote, and I wrote, and then I wrote again. These days, after every book, I say, "Well, I'm never doing that again." And my husband humors me, saying, "Okay, no problem. If you don't want to you don't have to." But eventually we both know I'll soon get itchy. (At least that's how it's been so far.) Creative work is essential to my well-being.

CYNTHIA LEITICH SMITH: When you look back on your enormously successful career, is there anything you would've done differently? If so, what and why? If not, how do you manage to move forward without regrets?

JUDY BLUME: My grown son tells me I'm the least analytical person he knows. Maybe that's not all bad. Maybe it's worked for me. I don't analyze my writing or my career. My first and longtime agent (sadly, she died several years ago) told me I was an intuitive writer. For better or worse, I think she was saying I just go with it, go where my characters take me. I tend not to get bogged down in the regrets department. I do the best I can. Not every book is for every reader. There's no way I'm ever going to satisfy everyone. (This is interesting because in my family I often feel I'm always trying to please everyone.)

CYNTHIA LEITICH SMITH: You have a color-ful and extensive Web site about yourself and your work, which I'm sure encourages ever more young readers to write you with their thoughts. You have published a book of letters before, but I wonder . . . Do the kids still write about the same kinds of things? Are there new issues on their minds today? Do they express themselves differently via e-mail than they did when the only means was paper and pen?

JUDY BLUME: The Web site has grown with the number of requests for info from students (from elementary school through grad school) doing papers on either censorship or my books. I joke that it's become an encyclopedia, that it's taken on a life of its own—but it sure beats trying to answer all those questions individually (which had become impossible anyway). George, my husband, designed it, built it, and helps me maintain it, but it still requires more time than either of us has and I'm always fretting, thinking I really have to make more time for it. It's the best way of keeping in touch with my readers!

I love e-mail! I love the immediacy of it. But I do think it tends to be less personal. It doesn't feel as private as sitting down with paper and pencil and baring your soul. I've had many fewer e-mails about really serious issues in kids' lives than when they were writing via snail mail. I still get snail mail letters (I'm not talking about the letters kids in class write as exercises, but deeply personal letters) and I've had some very seriously troubled kids contact me via e-mail.

CYNTHIA LEITICH SMITH: You have given so much over the course of your career. What are your goals for the future? Do you have another story on the boiling pot?

JUDY BLUME: All I know is that I have to be involved in some kind of creative project. Between books is a dangerous time for me. I begin to fantasize about all the things I could do to get out of starting another book. But what usually happens is, after a few months I can't stand it anymore and I start scribbling in my notebook. I keep a lot of ideas on the back burner—some have been there for years. I may never write those books but I like the security of knowing they're there.

Interview text reproduced with permission from Cynthia Leitich Smith, Copyright 2002, Cynthia Leitich Smith Children's Literature Resources, http://cynthialeitichsmith.com, http://www.cynthialeitichsmith.com/ auth-illJudyBlume.html

Timeline

1938 Judy Sussman is born on February 12, in Elizabeth, New Jersey.

1948–1949 Judy spends two years living in Miami Beach.

1952–1956 Judy attends an all-girls high school in New Jersey, where she edits the school newspaper, among other things.

1956 Judy begins an education degree at Boston University.

1957 Judy switches to New York University after a bout with mono.

1959 Rudolph Sussman, Judy's father, dies in July. Judy marries John Blume in August.

1960 Judy Blume receives a B.A. in education from New York University.

1961 Daughter Randy Lee is born.

1963 Son Lawrence (Larry) Andrew is born.

1966 Blume begins writing stories for children.

1967 Blume enrolls in a writing course for children at New York University.

1969 Blume's first book for children, *The One in the Middle is the Green Kangaroo*, is published.

1970 Blume's first two books for middle-g rade readers, *Iggie's House* and *Are You There God? It's Me, Margaret*, are published. *Margaret* is included on the *New York Times* list of outstanding books of the year, the first of many citations for Blume's books.

1971 *Freckle Juice* and *Then Again, Maybe I Won't* are published.

1972 *It's Not the End of the World, Tales of a Fourth Grade Nothing*, and *Otherwise Known as Sheila the Great* are published.

1973 *Deenie* is published.

1974 *Blubber* is published.

1975 Blume's first book for older readers, *Forever*, is published. Judy and John Blume divorce, and Judy and the children move to Princeton, New Jersey.

1976 Judy Blume marries Thomas Kitchens and moves to Los Alamos, New Mexico.

1977 *Starring Sally J. Freedman as Herself* is published.

1978 Blume's first book for adults, *Wifey*, is published.

1979 Blume and Thomas Kitchens divorce.

1980 *Superfudge* is published.

1981 *Tiger Eyes* is published. Blume establishes the KIDS Fund.

1983 *Smart Women* is published.

1984 *The Pain and the Great One* is published.

1985 Blume moves to New York City.

1986 *Letters to Judy: What Your Kids Wish They Could Tell You* is published.

1987 Blume marries George Cooper. Esther Sussman, Blume's mother, dies. *Just As Long As We're Together* is published.

1988 Blume writes and produces the film version of *Otherwise Known as Sheila the Great*.

1990 *Fudge-a-Mania* is published.

1993 *Here's to You, Rachel Robinson* is published.

1996 Blume receives one of the highest honors of her career, the Margaret A. Edwards Award for Lifetime Achievement from the American Library Association.

1998 *Summer Sister*s is published.

1999 Blume edits a collection of pieces about censorship called *Places I Never Meant to Be: Original Stories by Censored Writers*.

2002 *Double Fudge* is published.

Selected Reviews from *School Library Journal*

Double Fudge
2002

A worthy successor to *Superfudge* (1980) and *Fudge-a-Mania* (1990, both Dutton). Peter Hatcher is now entering seventh grade and apprehensive that no one will remember him since his family spent the past year in Princeton, New Jersey. Five-year-old Fudge is obsessed with money—acquiring it, talking and singing about it, and counting it. He even creates his own currency, Fudge Bucks. To try to curb this fixation, the family takes a trip to Washington, DC, to visit the Bureau of Printing and Engraving, and runs into Mr. Hatcher's long-lost cousin. Howie, his wife

Eudora, twin daughters Flora and Fauna, and four-year-old son Farley are traveling through the East Coast before moving to Florida. Of course, a visit to New York City is in their plans. A few weeks later, the relatives arrive and set out their sleeping bags. Two nights turn into four, then seven, and then Howie announces that he is subletting an apartment in the building for six weeks. It is a tough time for Peter, culminating at Halloween when Fudge and Farley are trapped in the building's elevator while trick-or-treating. Peter is a real twelve-year-old with all the insecurities and concerns of that age. And nothing can suppress the personality of Fudge, who even renames Washington, Fudgington.

Fudge-a-Mania
1990

The Tubmans and the Hatchers return in this latest chronicle of the hilarious escapades of Fudge, Pete, and Tootsie Hatcher and Sheila "Queen of Cooties" Tubman. Their parents decide to spend their summer vacation in the woods of Maine right next door to each other—but "next door" turns out to be in the same house. Fast-paced mayhem becomes the order of the day as children, adults (including Grandma Hatcher and Grandpa

Tubman), and assorted pets find themselves in daily (hourly?) predicaments. Not to be outdone in the madcap pace, Grandma and Grandpa announce their intention to be married. The story concludes with the solemn pact between Pete and Sheila that even though they'll be related, they will always hate each other. The story is filled with humor, and the upbeat mood is sustained at a hectic pace from first page to last. The uncomplicated plot is developed smoothly with just the right doses of surprise and laughter to keep readers turning the pages. Characters are credible, and never lose their identities. Be forewarned—fun between the covers of the bright red dust jacket means multiple copies for purchase.

Here's to You, Rachel Robinson
1993

This is the second book in what will likely become a trilogy revolving around three thirteen-year-old friends, Stephanie, Rachel, and Alison. In *Just As Long As We're Together* (Orchard, 1987), Stephanie described the turmoils of the first half of seventh grade. Here, Rachel picks up the narrative. Her intelligence and drive have always set her apart, and now her emotions are in a state of turbulence. The unwelcome return of her rebellious brother from boarding school unsettles her family, which is dominated by the intense and highly successful Mrs. Robinson. Charles wreaks havoc through his volatile behavior and cruel, but often insightful, attacks on his sisters and parents. Rachel also struggles to find a balance at school, where increasing pressures threaten to overwhelm her. While dealing with these concerns, she becomes attracted to an older man and longs for her peers to accept her. A master at conveying the values and mores of the upper-middle class, Blume excels in her descriptions of family life and adolescent friendships. Her characterization is powerful and compelling. Rachel's strong narrative voice, couched in simple, direct language, realistically conveys her intense self-preoccupation. Though Rachel is an unusual personality, the author never loses sight of the common threads running through the lives of all teenagers. She draws on the universal themes of awakening sexuality and emerging identities to capture and hold her audience. Preteens will snap this one up.

Superfudge
1980

Gr 4–6—No one knows the byways of the under-twelves better than Blume and that alone puts her ahead of the competition. Sixth-grader Peter Hatcher (*Tales of a Fourth Grade Nothing*, Dutton, 1972) plays a likeable straight man to his irrepressible little brother, Beezus to Fudgie's Ramona. Fudge won't budge from the bathroom the day Peter overindulges in Island Punch. Fudge papers baby Tootsie with green stamps ("I want to trade her in for a two-wheeler"). His first day at kindergarten, Fudge kicks and name-calls his uptight teacher. For this he gets an on-the-spot transfer to with-it Ms. Ziff's class. Blume lets her heroes off easy. Peter, who packs his Adidas bag in protest over a trial move from New York to (Princeton) New Jersey, is brushed, not bruised, by new experiences. The Hatchers (and supporting cast) don't have dimensions; they have attitudes. Smooth and easy to swallow, *Superfudge* is like a lemon meringue pie—without the lemon.

Tiger Eyes
1981

Gr 7–10—Adam Wexler was a loving family man but not one to plan ahead. When he's gunned down in his Atlantic City 7-Eleven store, his savings-and-insurance-less survivors are low on capital and resolve, a fatal combination. The fifteen-year-old-heroine, Davey, takes to her bed for two weeks and hyperventilates in school. Mom gives up and takes Davey and Jason, seven, to Los Alamos, the Bomb City, where Mr. Wexler's sister and her weapons designer husband live. Walter and Bitsy leave nothing to chance: they're believers in bicycle helmets, bomb shelters and bran flakes. Bitsy bakes cookies for an appreciative Jason and takes charge of her "instant family" while Mom sinks deeper into dependency and Davey chafes at unfamiliar restrictions and demands (getting C's without really trying is good enough for her but not for her uncle). In one of her resentful snits Davey runs into Wolf, a Hispanic heartthrob in hiking boots whose father just happens to be the terminal cancer patient Davey is drawn to on her candy striper rounds. Davey doesn't get Wolf in the end, but Mom recovers enough to start over in New Jersey. Despite her preoccupation with perspiration and blisters at her father's funeral, Davey's grief for him is the truest and best thing in the book. This isn't the most profound book about death around—it's skin deep where Fox's *A Place Apart* (Farrar, 1980) cuts to the bone—but with its be-easy-on-yourself sentiments it's certain to be one of the most popular.

List of
Selected Works

Are You There God? It's Me, Margaret.
Englewood Cliffs, NJ: Bradbury
Press, 1970.
Blubber. Scarsdale, NY: Bradbury Press, 1974.
Deenie. Scarsdale, NY: Bradbury Press, 1973.
Double Fudge. New York: Dutton, 2002.
Forever. Scarsdale, NY: Bradbury Press, 1975.
Freckle Juice. New York: Four Winds
Press, 1971.
Fudge-a-Mania. New York: Dutton, 1990.
Here's to You, Rachel Robinson. New York:
Orchard Books, 1993.
Iggie's House. Englewood Cliffs, NJ:
Bradbury Press, 1970.
It's Not the End of the World. Scarsdale, NY:
Bradbury Press, 1972.

Just As Long As We're Together. New York: Orchard Books, 1987.

Letters to Judy: What Kids Wish They Could Tell You. New York: Putnam, 1986.

The One in the Middle Is the Green Kangaroo. Englewood Cliffs, NJ: Bradbury Press, 1969.

Otherwise Known as Sheila the Great. New York: Dutton, 1972.

The Pain and the Great One. Scarsdale, NY: Bradbury Press, 1984.

Places I Never Meant to Be: Original Stories by Censored Writers. Edited by Judy Blume. New York: Simon & Schuster, 1999.

Starring Sally J. Freedman as Herself. Scarsdale, NY: Bradbury Press, 1977.

Superfudge. New York: Dutton, 1980.

Tales of a Fourth Grade Nothing. New York: Dutton, 1972.

Then Again, Maybe I Won't. Englewood Cliffs, NJ: Bradbury Press, 1971.

Tiger Eyes. Scarsdale, NY: Bradbury Press, 1981.

List of
Selected Awards

Margaret A. Edwards Award for Lifetime Achievement from the American Library Association (1996)

Are You There God? It's Me, Margaret (1970)

Great Stone Face Award, New Hampshire Library Association (1980)

Nene Award from the Children of Hawaii (1975)

North Dakota Children's Choice Book Award (1979)

Outstanding Book of the Year, *New York Times* (1970)

Young Hoosier Award, Indiana Media Educators (1976)

Blubber (1974)

North Dakota Children's Choice Book Award (1983)

Outstanding Book of the Year, *New York Times* (1974)

***Freckle Juice* (1971)**
Michigan Young Readers' Award, Michigan Council of Teachers (1980)

***Fudge-a-Mania* (1990)**
California Young Reader Medal (1993)
Nene Award from the Children of Hawaii (1993)

***Here's to You, Rachel Robinson* (1993)**
Parents' Choice Award, Parents' Choice Foundation (1993)

***Just as Long as We're Together* (1987)**
Young Readers' List, Virginia State Reading Association (1989)

***Otherwise Known as Sheila the Great* (1972)**
Book of the Month Award, German Academy for Children's and Young People's Literature (1984)
South Carolina Children's Book Award (1978)
South Carolina Children's Book Award (1982)

***The Pain and the Great One* (1984)**
Children's Choices, International Reading Association and Children's Book Council Committee (1985)
Young Readers' Choice Award, Alabama Library Association (1986)

Superfudge (1980)

California Young Reader Medal (1983)

Children's Choice Award, International
Reading Association and Children's Book
Council (1981)

International Reading and Library
Association (1984)

Nene Award from the Children of Hawaii (1982)

New Mexico Land of Enchantment Children's
Book Award, New Mexico (1984)

Texas Bluebonnet Award (1980)

Texas Bluebonnet Award (1982)

Young Readers' Choice Award, Pacific
Northwest Library Association, Edmonton,
Alberta, Canada (1983)

Tales of a Fourth Grade Nothing (1972)

Massachusetts Children's Book Award (1983)

Pacific Northwest Library Association Young
Readers' Choice (1975)

West Australian Young Readers' Book
Award (1980)

Tiger Eyes (1981)

A Best Book for Young Adults, *School Library
Journal* (1981)

Books for the Teen Age, New York Public
Library (1982)

California Young Reader Medal (1983)

Glossary

advocate To support or defend.

apathetic Having no feeling, emotion, or interest.

arbitrary Chosen by chance or impulse and not by reason or need.

bohemian Living an unconventional life, usually as an artist or writer.

catapult To launch.

censorship When material (such as books) is suppressed because someone decides it is offensive.

class Economic or social status.

hypochondriac Someone who suffers from imaginary physical ailments.

moralize To offer a judgment about whether something is right or wrong.

myth A popular belief that is actually imaginary.

naive Innocent and not very wise.

Nazism The political and economic beliefs regarding racial superiority that were put into practice in Germany during the first half of the twentieth century.

objectionable Undesirable or offensive.

pan To give a negative review, as a critic.

patented Having a patent or an official registration.

racial discrimination The judgment of someone as inferior on the basis of his or her skin color or culture.

role model A person whose behavior in a particular role is imitated by others.

scoliosis Curvature of the spine.

sleeper Something that is slow to become popular.

suppress To keep from being shown.

verge To be on the edge.

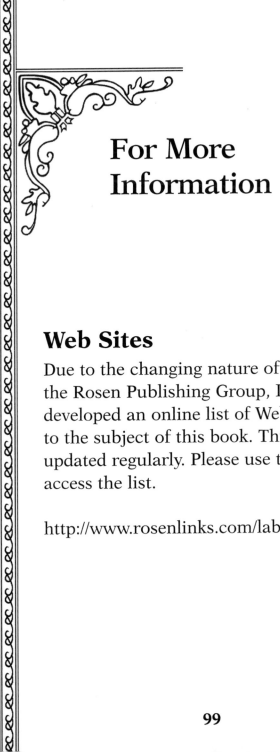

For More Information

Web Sites

Due to the changing nature of Internet links, the Rosen Publishing Group, Inc., has developed an online list of Web sites related to the subject of this book. This site is updated regularly. Please use this link to access the list.

http://www.rosenlinks.com/lab/jblu

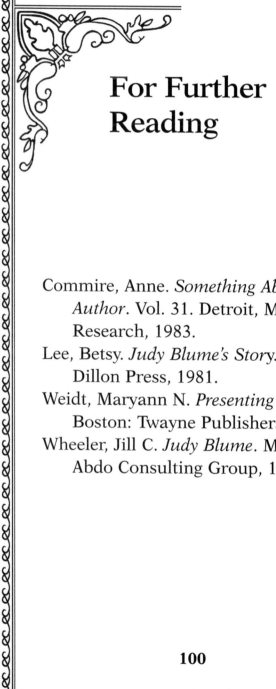

For Further Reading

Commire, Anne. *Something About the Author*. Vol. 31. Detroit, MI: Gale Research, 1983.

Lee, Betsy. *Judy Blume's Story*. Minneapolis: Dillon Press, 1981.

Weidt, Maryann N. *Presenting Judy Blume*. Boston: Twayne Publishers, 1990.

Wheeler, Jill C. *Judy Blume*. Minneapolis: Abdo Consulting Group, 1996.

Bibliography

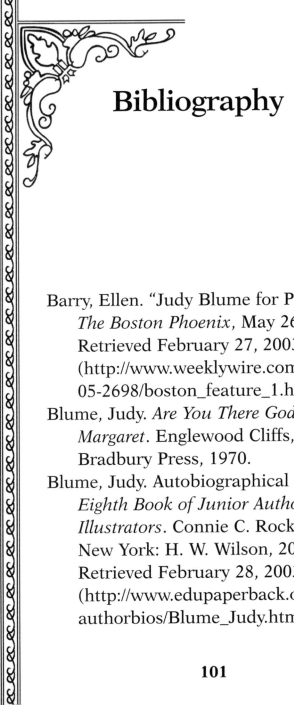

Barry, Ellen. "Judy Blume for President."
    The Boston Phoenix, May 26, 1998.
    Retrieved February 27, 2003
    (http://www.weeklywire.com/ww/
    05-2698/boston_feature_1.html).

Blume, Judy. *Are You There God? It's Me,
    Margaret*. Englewood Cliffs, NJ:
    Bradbury Press, 1970.

Blume, Judy. Autobiographical statement.
    *Eighth Book of Junior Authors and
    Illustrators*. Connie C. Rockman, ed.
    New York: H. W. Wilson, 2000.
    Retrieved February 28, 2003
    (http://www.edupaperback.org/
    authorbios/Blume_Judy.html).

Blume, Judy. *Blubber*. Scarsdale, NY: Bradbury Press, 1974.

Blume, Judy. *Deenie*. Scarsdale, NY: Bradbury Press, 1973.

Blume, Judy. *Forever*. Scarsdale, NY: Bradbury Press, 1975.

Blume, Judy. *Letters to Judy: What Your Kids Wish They Could Tell You*. New York: Putnam, 1986.

Blume, Judy, ed. *Places I Never Meant to Be: Original Stories by Censored Writers*. New York: Simon & Schuster, 1999. Retrieved March 3, 2003 (http://judyblume.com/articles/places-intro.html).

Blume, Judy. "1975 Sequoyah Award Acceptance Speech." *Oklahoma Librarian*, October 1975, p. 7.

Blume, Judy. *Starring Sally J. Freedman as Herself*. Scarsdale, NY: Bradbury Press, 1977.

Blume, Judy. *Then Again, Maybe I Won't*. Englewood Cliffs, NJ: Bradbury Press, 1971.

Blume, Judy. "What Kids Want to Read." *Principal*, January 1982.

Blume, Judy, and Jennifer Baumgardner. "How Did You Manage a Writing Career While Raising Kids?" Anna Bondoc and Anna and Meg Daly, eds. *Letters of Intent: Women*

Cross the Generations to Talk About Family, Work, Sex, Love and the Future of Feminism. New York: The Free Press, 1999.

Carr Library. "Judy Blume." Retrieved February 28, 2003 (http://ccpl.carr.org/mae/blume/blume.htm).

Commire, Anne, ed. *Something About the Author.* Vol. 31. Detroit, MI: Gale Research, 1983.

Dillin, Gay Andrews. "Judy Blume: Children's Author in a Grown-Up Controversy." *The Christian Science Monitor,* December 29, 1981, pp. B4–B5.

Gallo, Don. "What Should Teachers Know About YA Lit for 2004?" *English Journal,* November 1984, pp. 31–34.

Haas, Diane. Review of *Starring Sally J. Freedman as Herself, School Library Journal,* May 1977.

Internet School Library Media Centre. "Judy Blume Teacher Resource File." Retrieved March 1, 2003 (http://falcon.jmu.edu/~ramseyil/blume.htm).

Judy Blume's Home Base. Retrieved March 5, 2003 (http://judyblume.com).

Kanner, Ellen. "A Woman for All Seasons Reflects on Growing Up and Growing

Older." *Bookpage: America's Book Review*, May 1998. Retrieved March 5, 2003 (http://www.bookpage.com/9805bp/ judy_blume.html).

Lee, Betsy. *Judy Blume's Story*. Minneapolis: Dillon Press, 1981.

Marley, Kate. "An Interview with Judy Blume." *Baltimore's Child*, July/August 1986. Retrieved March 3, 2003 (http://www.secondstarttotheright.com/ books/column/c786.htm).

Mercier, Jean. Review of *Starring Sally J. Freedman as Herself, Publishers Weekly*, April 18, 1977, p. 62.

Oppenheimer, Mark. "Why Judy Blume Endures." *New York Times Book Review*, November 16, 1997. Retrieved February 15, 2003 (http://judyblume.com/articles/ oppenheimer.html).

Power, Jane. "Meet Judy Blume; Kid's-Eye View Draws Students . . . and Censors." *NEA Today*, October 1984, pp. 10–11.

Random House. "Judy Blume." Retrieved March 3, 2003 (http://www.randomhouse.com/ teachers/authors/blum.html).

Review of *Otherwise Known as Sheila the Great, Kirkus Reviews*, September 1, 1972, p. 1,025.

Review of *Superfudge*. *New York Times Book Review*. Retrieved March 2003 (http://judyblume.com/superfudge.html).

Review of *Tales of a Fourth Grade Nothing*. *Publishers Weekly*. Retrieved February 17, 2003 (http://judyblume.com/tales.html).

Scholastic. "About the Author." Retrieved March 5, 2003 (http://www2.scholastic.com/teachers/authorsandbooks/authorstudies/authorhom.jhtml?authorID=11).

Weidt, Maryann N. *Presenting Judy Blume*. Boston: Twayne Publishers, 1990.

Wheeler, Jill C. *Judy Blume*. Minneapolis: Abdo Consulting Group, 1996.

Wintle, Justin, and Emma Fisher, eds. "Judy Blume." *The Pied Pipers: Interviews with the Influential Creators of Children's Literature*. New York: Paddington Press, 1975.

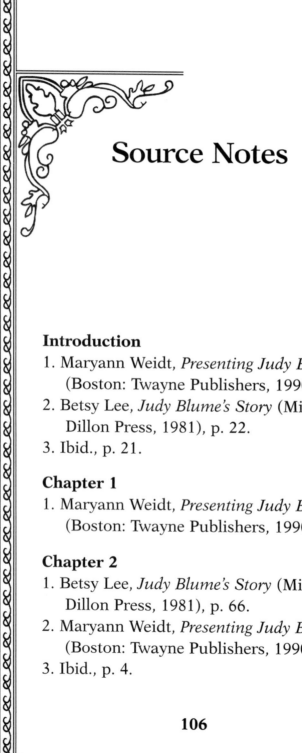

Source Notes

Introduction

1. Maryann Weidt, *Presenting Judy Blume* (Boston: Twayne Publishers, 1990), p. 58.
2. Betsy Lee, *Judy Blume's Story* (Minneapolis: Dillon Press, 1981), p. 22.
3. Ibid., p. 21.

Chapter 1

1. Maryann Weidt, *Presenting Judy Blume* (Boston: Twayne Publishers, 1990), p. 13.

Chapter 2

1. Betsy Lee, *Judy Blume's Story* (Minneapolis: Dillon Press, 1981), p. 66.
2. Maryann Weidt, *Presenting Judy Blume* (Boston: Twayne Publishers, 1990), p. 11.
3. Ibid., p. 4.

4. Lee, p. 92.
5. Ibid., pp. 93–94.
6. Judy Blume, autobiographical statement, *Eighth Book of Junior Authors and Illustrators* (New York: H. W. Wilson, 2000).

Chapter 3
1. Betsy Lee, *Judy Blume's Story* (Minneapolis: Dillon Press, 1981), p. 98.
2. Judy Blume, *Then Again, Maybe I Won't* (Englewood Cliffs, NJ: Bradbury Press, 1971), pp. 99–100.
3. Judy Blume, *Deenie* (Scarsdale, NY: Bradbury Press, 1973), p. 53.
4. Ibid., p. 71.
5. Anne Commire, ed., *Something About the Author*, Vol. 31 (Detroit: Gale Research, 1983), p. 31.
6. Blume, *Deenie*, pp. 91–92.
7. Ibid., pp. 92–93.
8. Mark Oppenheimer, "Why Judy Blume Endures," *New York Times Book Review*, November 16, 1997.
9. Justin Wintle and Emma Fisher, eds., "Judy Blume," *The Pied Pipers: Interviews with the Influential Creators of Children's Literature* (New York: Paddington Press, 1975), p. 320.

Chapter 4
1. Maryann Weidt, *Presenting Judy Blume* (Boston:

Twayne Publishers, 1990), p. 8.

2. Judy Blume, *Forever* (Scarsdale, NY: Bradbury Press, 1975), p. 93.

3. *New York Times Book Review*. Review of *Forever*, December 28, 1975, p. 20.

Chapter 5

1. Judy Blume, "Introduction," *Places I Never Meant to Be: Original Stories by Censored Writers*, (New York: Simon & Schuster, 1999).

2. *Newsletter on Intellectual Freedom*, January 1983, p. 21.

3. Judy Blume, *Blubber* (Scarsdale, NY: Bradbury Press, 1974), p. 89.

4. Blume, "Introduction," *Places I Never Meant to Be: Original Stories by Censored Writers*.

5. Ibid.

6. *Principal*, "What Kids Want to Read," Volume 61, Number 3, January 1982, pp. 6–7.

7. Kate Marley, "An Interview with Judy Blume," *Baltimore's Child*, July/August 1986.

Chapter 6

1. Maryann Weidt, *Presenting Judy Blume* (Boston: Twayne Publishers, 1990), p. 18.

2. Don Gallo, "What Should Teachers Know About YA Lit for 2004?" *English Journal*, November 1984, p. 32.

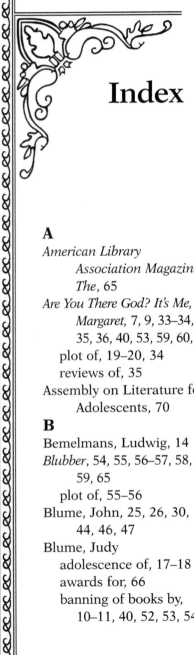

Index

109

About the Author

Cee Telford is a freelance writer living in Toronto.

Photo Credits

Cover and p. 2 © Bettmann/Corbis

Series Designer: Tahara Hasan; Editor: Annie Sommers